PASSPORT TO HEAVEN

Louis Petrossi

ISBN 979-8-89345-006-4 (paperback)
ISBN 979-8-89345-007-1 (hardcover)
ISBN 979-8-89345-008-8 (digital)

Christian Faith Publishing
832 Park Avenue
Meadville, PA 16335
www.christianfaithpublishing.com

Printed in the United States of America

I dedicate this book to my six children: Tiffany, Mary, Susan, Louis Jr., Melanie, and Frank.

I also dedicate this story to my eleven grandchildren: Gabriella, Liam, Aidan, Lily, Emma, Kate, Addison, Jack, Jonathan, Stephanie, and Lexi.

Preface

Passport to Heaven sprouted from a conversation between an eleven-year-old girl and her grandfather. Even though the young girl's mother died during childbirth, God had blessed her with a positive outlook on life. Her mother's deep faith in God, combined with her grandfather's loving care, created the wonderful young lady portrayed in this story. *Passport to Heaven* illuminates a path for all people of all ages and beliefs to achieve a legacy of goodwill. At the center, *Passport to Heaven* guides us to a fulfilling life by helping us to practice four basic principles espoused in the Bible: gratitude, loyalty, forgiveness, and sharing. The beauty of the *Passport to Heaven* lies in emphasizing and documenting the little actions we can take daily. After all, the little things we do have the largest impact on each person. *Passport to Heaven* tells us a beautiful story. The story leads us to a way of bringing joy into the lives of those around us. By spreading joy to others, we experience the greatest happiness, satisfaction, and reward from life.

Passport to Heaven

Eleven-year-old Mary always felt happy, despite never experiencing the nurturing love of her mother, who passed away during a complicated birth delivery. Mary, however, did inherit her mother's natural joy for life, vivacious appetite for knowledge, and, most importantly, her absolute faith in God. Mary truly enjoyed the time she spent with her grandpa Leone. He always fed her hungry and inquisitive mind and encouraged her to think independently. In return, Grandpa Leone loved his granddaughter more than life itself. Mary reminded him of his deceased daughter in mannerisms, facial expressions, unyielding happiness, and staunch faith. They both relished their conversations, mostly initiated by Mary's profound and insightful questions about God.

During one of those conversations, Mary, as she often did, asked Grandpa Leone a question that he never thought deeply about.

Mary asked, "Grandpa, will I need a passport to get into heaven when the time comes?"

Grandpa Leone, taken quite by surprise and wonderment, smiled at Mary and asked, "What made you think of that, Mary? That's a very interesting question."

"Well, Grandpa," Mary replied, "don't we need a passport to travel to a different country? If heaven is a place we travel to somewhere in the universe like earth, wouldn't I need a passport to get in and be with my mother?"

Baffled yet fascinated, Grandpa thought about the question, while praying for inspiration. While Grandpa thought, Mary patiently settled in, excited and anticipating his response.

Finally, he said, "Mary, God answered your question in the Bible, in the Lord's Prayer, the Our Father. It says, 'Thy kingdom come; it will be done on earth as it is in heaven.' So I am certain that heaven is most likely a place much like earth. I agree we may need a very special passport to get to heaven. I also believe your mother in heaven is waiting for you when your time on earth comes to an end. I'm sure your mother still watches over you and guides you. As you know, Mary, God's only son, Jesus, by His life, death, and resurrection, bestowed the opportunity for eternal life in the kingdom of God to all humans on earth. In return, He asked that we live our life based on very modest principles. The passport to heaven does provide a simple but profound guide to help us follow God's wishes and illuminates the path to the kingdom of God."

Mary beamed with excitement and awe. "Grandpa, I am very excited! I certainly am willing to do whatever I must do to please God so I may be with my mother in heaven and also be a better person on earth. Please tell me what I must do!"

Grandpa smiled at Mary. "On your passport to heaven, it provides a place to record all of your good deeds during your life on earth. Your mother knows you will be with her when you follow the teachings of the Lord. Your mother gladly and lovingly gave her life so you could live and experience God's gift of life on earth, knowing that one day you would be with her for eternity. When the doctor told your mother in the hospital that he could not save both of you, your mom said, 'Please save my daughter's life. I will be in fine in the Lord's hands.'

"Your mother's absolute faith provided the strength and serenity to make that difficult decision. She knew God would watch over you and keep you safe."

"Grandpa, I would not be here with you today if my mother did not do that, but I am sad she had to die so that I could live. Having you here with me proves that God really is watching over me. I love you so much, Grandpa!"

"Mary, your mother had complete faith in God, and like all mothers, she placed your life ahead of her life because she loved you so much. I was also there in the hospital when you were born. Your mother was always a kind, loving person to all people. Your mother knew, in her heart, soul, and mind, that you and she would be united together eventually in heaven for all eternity. Her decision proved her absolute courage, unquestioning faith, infinite hope, and boundless love. Mary, you are a very special gift from God, like all people on earth."

"Grandpa, I can feel my mother's love in my heart and God's love in my soul. I want to follow Jesus and the way He taught us to live. I love Jesus the same way I love you and my mother, so I need to work on my passport so I can get to heaven."

"Mary, your mother wanted you to enjoy life on earth and then in heaven. Our lives pass very quickly on earth, but the kingdom of God lasts forever."

"How do I get my passport to heaven?"

"You began your journey on the day you were baptized and continue it because you love God above all else. Anyone can follow that path and start their own passport to heaven. God's laws are fair and just and apply to all people equally. In fact, heaven and earth could disappear, but God's laws and teachings can never be overturned."

"Grandpa, I already love God, and I always will."

"That's perfect, Mary. The passport to heaven helps us keep track of our good deeds. We move closer to God whenever we follow his teachings. The more we do, the better our life on earth becomes for everyone around us."

"Heaven must be a beautiful place. What would it be like, Grandpa?"

"You're right, Mary. Heaven is the promised paradise. Heaven emanates love, beauty, happiness and peace. Everyone in heaven respects each other. Nobody experiences anger, jealously, hatred, pain or suffering. God's infinite love courses through every soul in heaven."

Grandpa's description captivated Mary. "Wow! That really is like paradise."

"Yes, it is! God made heaven as a gift to all humanity and gave Jesus, his only Son, so that everyone on earth had the opportunity to enjoy His gifts for all of eternity."

"So how do I use my passport to heaven, Grandpa?"

"On your passport to heaven, there are four different stamps and markings, like the ink stamps put on your personal passport when you visit other countries on earth. The passport to heaven covers four virtues: gratitude, loyalty, forgiveness, and sharing. Every time you perform a good deed, you simply record it by writing it down on your own passport to heaven. The number of times you help others using the virtues in the passport to heaven determines your path into the kingdom of heaven. When your time on earth ends, your personal passport to heaven will show all of your good deeds. Also, while you travel through life, you can document and reflect on all of your accomplishments for others and self."

"Sort of like grades in school, Grandpa. I want to get an A plus on my passport to heaven. What should I do next?"

"Do at least one good deed every day, or as much as possible, from each of the four virtues in the passport to heaven and write them down on your passport as you do them. If you really feel special about something that you've done or experienced, you can write about it, like a legacy. The more you help others, the more good deed markings you will record on your passport to heaven. Gratitude, loyalty, forgiveness, and sharing are very important and the secret to a fulfilling and joyful life. Going to heaven rewards us more than anything on earth. So let's look at the first virtue in the passport to heaven."

Gratitude

"Gratitude shows God our humility," replied Grandpa. "When we respect those around us and all of God's blessings given to us, we express gratitude. Be thankful, Mary, for all the good in your life and don't focus all your time on wanting more."

"Praying to God tells Him how grateful I am for everything. So I'm going to make sure I thank God every morning when I wake up and every night before I go to sleep. Also, I'll try real hard to notice God's gifts to me during the day, not just big gifts but the little ones too."

"Excellent, Mary! You really have a good grasp and understand exactly what gratitude represents. Many times we overlook the little parts of our everyday lives and take them for granted. Appreciating everything around you embodies the real meaning of gratitude. Never forget to thank those around you too. Remember, saying 'Thank you' brings happiness, a feeling of appreciation, and joy to other people. God, in His infinite wisdom, chose gratitude as an important virtue for two reasons—first, being grateful to others warms their hearts because it lets them know they have helped someone, and more importantly, being grateful shows God that we humble ourselves in His presence. Essentially, Mary, showing gratitude to people and to God lets them know you appreciate them."

"That's amazing and wonderful, Grandpa! I know exactly what I will do to show God my gratitude. I will pray to Him every day to tell Him about my faith in Him and the hope He has given to me. I will express that faith and hope by showing others how grateful I am to them. I love God more than anything. He created me and the miracle of the universe that surrounds me. By showing my gratitude, God will see that I put Him first and that I belong in the kingdom of heaven with my mother."

"Well spoken, Mary. Gratitude for the faith and hope which God's unconditional love gave us lasts forever. God bestowed His love on us to let us prosper. Faith and hope tells us believing in them makes anything possible. Mary, our love of Jesus opens all doors to every blessing we will ever need. Jesus anchors us so steadfastly that we can weather any storm in our lives. Always be grateful that Jesus absolutely stands with us no matter what happens. He knows we can overcome any challenge with Him in our corner."

"Jesus gives us the gift of success! I don't mean money, Grandpa, I mean success in our life. He knows us much better than we can ever know ourselves."

Grandpa, beaming with pride, replied, "The Lord knows where we may fail. In His greatness, He gave us the ability to go forward by honoring His teachings for a life well lived. Gratitude touches every aspect of our life. Thank God for having food, water, sunlight, a place to live, and even the clothes we wear. Also, thank Him for allowing us to spread His word and His joy through gratitude. Most of all, thank Him for blessing us with the gift of being alive to help others by following His teachings. I am certain you will earn many markings in your passport to heaven for gratitude every day of your life. Write the ones important to you in the passport to heaven. Your life will improve every day, and Jesus will see your thoughts and actions. You will make Him proud, and He won't forget your gratitude good deeds."

Seeing Mary's broad smile and unfaltering attention, Grandpa added, "I am sure you already show the Lord your gratitude and will continue to do so every day, adding to your markings in the gratitude section of your passport to heaven. The kingdom of God gets closer when gratitude fills your heart."

"Thank you, Grandpa. I love the way you teach and can't wait to hear the rest."

Loyalty

"Mary, no matter what happens in our life, God will never forsake us. God bestows His gifts of loyalty upon us. By returning God's gift of loyalty to Him, we spread that gift to others."

"I am not sure I understand, Grandpa." Mary responded with a slightly puzzled look on her face.

"God teaches all of us by His words and His living example. Our purpose requires that we not only listen carefully to God's words but also observe God's actions very closely. The scriptures give us many examples about God's loyalty to us. When God sacrificed His only Son, Jesus, so we could be forgiven of our sins, He demonstrated the ultimate and most beautiful gift of loyalty for us to enter the kingdom of heaven."

"Was it my mother's decision to go to heaven so that I could live and experience her loyalty to me?" she questioned her grandpa.

Grandpa's eyes teared up with pride as he felt incredibly blessed to have both a wonderful daughter and granddaughter.

"Yes, Mary, she did. But remember, Mary, the little acts of loyalty you demonstrate on a daily basis pave our path to heaven. The passport to heaven keeps reminding us by recording and writing down our loyalty deeds every day."

Mary thought of the biblical story of the lost sheep. She said, "The Lord is our shepherd, and we are his beloved sheep. There is nothing we lack. The Lord will watch over us and bring us back when we stray away. I know that no matter what we do in our life, the Lord will always be loyal to us."

Grandpa liked Mary's thinking and exclaimed, "*Exactly!* When we show our loyalty to God by being loyal to those around us, He will lead us back to the right path when we stray. He is our Savior. Let's learn how we can show our loyalty to those around us. Loyal friends support us in our life pursuits and in our daily struggles. You can always ask a loyal friend for help when the going gets tough. They willingly and happily help in any way that you may need their help. Why? Loyal friends help unconditionally. They freely give their time, support, generosity and kindness. Unselfish loyalty is the way to act."

Mary's eyes widened, and her face reflected her wonderment and focus on Grandpa's words.

He continued, "Loyal friends support you when others treat you badly. Loyal friends stand by your side both in good times and in bad times. They never exhibit pettiness, envy, or jealously. You can count on them when you need their support."

"Grandpa, you have taught me a lot about loyalty. Now I can learn more by watching my loyal friends!" exclaimed Mary.

"That's a good way to proceed, Mary. Moreover, loyal friends give each other complete freedom to be themselves. Just like God has given us free will, we show our loyalty to others by accepting them the way they are. When they feel pain and sorrow, let them share it with you, without judging them, and listen carefully to what concerns then. Above all, be honest in your dealing with all people. Your honesty and caring will impact them the most and encourage them to be loyal to you also. God, in His infinite wisdom, teaches us to courageously face the truth. We gain our courage through the serenity prayer. It is a beautiful prayer, full of wisdom and profound understanding, that says, 'Grant us the serenity to accept the things we cannot change, the courage to change the things we can, and the wisdom to know the difference.' It has helped me cope with adversity immensely over my lifetime."

"I think I understand better now, Grandpa. We have to be honest and truthfully face all situations. People will feel our loyalty to them when we stand by them and help them overcome difficulties in their life, no matter how small. Being loyal means we treat their difficulties with respect. We stand by them and help them weather the storm until it passes and peaceful blue skies return."

"Yes, Mary. I am so proud of you! Loyalty brings comfort and joy to others just like God's loyalty envelops our life in a soft, warm blanket of safety and security. Following the wisdom, empathy, and compassion in the serenity prayer faithfully and honestly provides us the strength we need to be loyal to others and ourselves. I can see you love for God helps you understand so well. That love will guide your path to the kingdom of heaven."

"Grandpa. I have a suggestion."

"What is it?"

"Well, I have learned so much from you today! Can we go get some ice cream?"

"Of course," Grandpa said, laughing. "I believe God would love to see us enjoy some ice cream. I know I certainly will."

About a week later

Mary had a fun week. Mostly she thought about what she and her grandfather talked about gratitude and loyalty. She couldn't help smiling about everything she had learned. Her young, absorbent brain and her heart, overflowing with love for God and her faith, longed to learn more from her grandpa.

"Grandpa?" she asked. "Is it time to keep going?"

Grandpa playfully grinned and acted like he was thinking about it. Then he replied, "Mary your enthusiasm warms my heart so much. So let's move on to the next virtue."

Forgiveness

"Mary," Grandpa began, "the next virtue in the passport to heaven may be the most difficult."

As usual, Mary settled in next to Grandpa, excitedly anticipating what she would learn today.

"Let's talk about forgiveness. Scripture tells us if we forgive those who sin against us, God will forgive our sins. God emphasized *forgiveness* because when we forgive, we bestow a great gift on someone. God gave all of us that gift by offering His only Son, Jesus, to every one of us on earth as a path to God's *forgiveness*."

Mary chimed in, "The strength given to me by God's love and knowing that His love overcomes everything inspires me to freely forgive those who may have harmed me. Also, by forgiving others, I will feel God's love even more!"

"Mary, every time we talk, I only become more proud and amazed!"

"Thank you, Grandpa. Please tell me more about *forgiveness*."

"As you so smartly pointed out, *forgiveness* makes others feel better as much as it makes us feel better. We all fail and make mistakes that can hurt other people. Mary, only God never fails to do what is right and avoid what is wrong. We all have shortcomings in our life. God, by forgiving us, teaches the importance of *forgiveness*. People mostly try to be good and kind. When we fail, we often feel bad about it. When we tell others it's okay, we help heal their hearts, and more importantly, we feel the power and serenity of *forgiveness*. When we don't forgive, we feel worse. We may even feel resentment or anger, which leads us farther away from God and blocks our right to happiness. We must pray to God for the courage to be humble and follow the Lord's guidance. By forgiving, we show God our humility by recognizing our own faults."

"I recall the other day, at school, someone cut in front of the line at lunch," Mary said to her grandpa. "At first, I became angry about it, Now, by forgiving him, I feel better about the whole incident, even if he doesn't know I forgave him. I can think of another time when a friend may have accidently done something to hurt me. When I said, 'I forgive you,' we both felt happy. God really knows the positive power of *forgiveness*. I am so thankful to the Lord for teaching us about forgiveness and how important *forgiveness* is for me."

"You are correct, Mary. We have to allow each other's faults and forgive each other. Saying 'I forgive you' and having faith in God will lead you and help you move on in your life in a positive direction. Pray to God to help you love all people in spite of what they did to you, even if what they did to you was a small thing. If we do wrong, just ask God to forgive us for hurting someone else. Forgive quickly and make it a part of you. Because *forgiveness* can be difficult, you'll learn that the more you do it, the easier it gets. God taught us *forgiveness* because He wants to make it an important part of our life on earth. You will want to mark down many notations for *forgiveness* in your passport to heaven, Mary."

"Amen, Grandpa."

Sharing

"The fourth virtue that we record in our passport to heaven comes from *sharing*. Mary, the sharing that Jesus teaches us about differs from the sharing you may think about, like sharing your toys. Jesus asks us to share ourselves, our time, our talents, and our love in the name of God. When we set our hearts to the task of sharing, we don't only help the people we share with, but we also please God and ourselves."

"Like God says, 'When you give to the poor, you are giving to me,'" replied Mary.

She agreed with her grandfather that *sharing* represents a very important part of our passport to heaven.

Mary added, "So many people around us have needs that they can't handle themselves. Doing what God teaches us and serving those people in need will please the Lord, won't it, Grandpa?"

"You said it perfectly, Mary. Giving rewards us more than getting. We can share feelings; give a compliment; give our time, or our money, or one of our possessions. Really, we share whatever someone may need for their comfort or suffering. Every day I try to acknowledge something a friend accomplished or congratulate someone on a birthday or anniversary. *Sharing* a little bit of our time can make a big difference in how another person can feel. People feel good when they know someone cares and appreciates them."

Mary continued her thoughts, saying, "I can give a warm smile or kind words to many people every day. I can text, email, and, of course, phone anyone who needs cheering up."

A tear fell from Grandpa's eyes as he wished his daughter could see the beautiful and thoughtful girt Mary had grown into. Then he smiled, knowing his beloved daughter was watching Mary develop into a beautiful person in many ways.

He told Mary, "If we praise and compliment people instead of condemning them, we will have a positive influence on many lives and make the world a better place.

"By the way, I took all the valuable things from my house that I no longer use or need and gave those things to people who really needed them. It saved a lot of money for those in need. My satisfaction and joy came from seeing the gratitude and smiles on their faces."

Mary made a list of what she could share and give to others in her mind. Her ideas easily rolled out.

"I need to not be selfish or hoard things, but think how I can help others in need, no matter what that need may be."

Grandpa encouragingly replied, "Mary, without a doubt, you will earn many markings for good deeds of sharing in your passport to heaven. Your wonderful and thoughtful ideas guarantee that! May God always bless and protect your tender heart. I know He will surely be pleased with you."

"Thank you, Grandpa. I know my mother in heaven smiles because she knows I'm with you now, and one day, we will all be together for ever and ever!"

Grandpa responded, "Your mother placed you in God's hands from the very moment you were born. Everyone must know that the kingdom of God can be reached by practicing the four virtues in the passport to heaven—*gratitude, loyalty, forgiveness, sharing*. Even though those four virtues embody the main attributes which guide our life, God gave them to us as building blocks to a completely fulfilling life and a pathway to his glory."

After Mary and Grandpa finished talking about the passport to heaven, Grandpa was excited. He smiled, winked at Mary, and said, "I have a very special gift for a very special girl."

"What is it, Grandpa?" asked Mary, full of enthusiasm.

Grandpa handed her a box and told her to open it.

When she opened it, Mary eyes opened extrawide in astonishment.

"Grandpa, it's my own passport to heaven with my name on it!"

"Yes, Mary. I know you will make good use of it for a long time."

"Thank you. Much thanks and appreciation, Grandpa," Mary exclaimed. Then she gave him a big hug and said, "I love you so much, Grandpa. My passport to heaven will bring me so much closer to God, and when He calls me, I'll definitely be ready to see my mother. I miss Mom dearly, but I am at peace waiting to join her in heaven." Mary leaned into Grandpa Leone's arms. She looked up and said, "The very first thought I am going to put in my passport to heaven will show how grateful I am for you and for my mother. You are the best grandpa in the world. I am a very blessed person."

Your Personal Passport
to Heaven

Name:_______________________________

Date:_______________________________

This Passport to Heaven gives us a concrete representation of a path we can take to enter the kingdom of heaven. The idea sprouted from an insightful question by an eleven-year-old child asked her grandfather. The discussion that followed defined how all of us can be better people, spread love and joy to others, and enter the kingdom of heaven.

Simply record your good deeds of gratitude, loyalty, forgiveness, and sharing in your Passport to Heaven, and God Almighty will be aware of them.

Passport to Heaven is your personal legacy to a life well-lived and everlasting happiness.

Passport to Heaven came into existence from a conversation between an eleven-year-old girl and her grandfather when she asked: "Do I need a passport to go to heaven and be with my mother." Even though the young girl's mother died during childbirth. God blessed her with a positive outlook on life. Her mother's deep faith in God, combined with her grandfather's loving care created the wonderful young lady portrayed in this story.

Passport to heaven illuminates a path for all people of all ages and beliefs to achieve a written legacy of good will. At its center, passport to heaven guides us to a fulfilling life by helping us to practice and to write down four basis virtues espoused in the Bible: gratitude, loyalty, forgiveness and sharing. Doing good deeds are always one of the most rewarding experiences for humankind. Each good deed recorded in your passport to heaven is also a path to the kingdom of heaven. For God takes notice of all good things we do and always stamps his approval on our good deeds.

Passport to heaven is a beautiful way for you to document the essence of a life well-lived and to do your part to bring understanding, kindness, love and peace to all people. By spreading joy to others, we experience the greatest happiness, satisfaction, and rewards in our life. Be sure to share the passport to heaven with family, friends, and associates at work. The purpose of passport to heaven touches all of us. Let the rest of your life be a legacy of the best of your life.

Gratitude

Loyalty

Forgiveness

Sharing

About the Author

The author has a passion for life. He was raised in Connecticut at a time when the family was a cohesive God-loving unit and where grandparents, aunts, uncles, cousins all lived nearby. He was blessed with many mentors and loved ones.

Later, to finance his college education, the author went to New York and joined the Merchant Marine. He sailed the seven seas for eight years, and that education was worth more to him than his bachelor's and master's degrees. His travels put him in touch with people from all cultures and walks of life in the Americas, Asia, and Europe. He studied various beliefs and philosophies but remained a loyal disciple of Jesus. He believes we are one people under one God, with love being the cornerstone of our life.

The author's career spans service as a schoolteacher, businessman, serial entrepreneur, and global seminar speaker to thousands of people on how to succeed in life. He is the author of *How Ordinary People Become Millionaires* and *The Richest Man in China*. For his charitable activities, he was inducted into the Knights of Malta, Order of St John. The author lived in China for two years; but his favorite place, away from his Nevada residence, is Italy where his grandparents came from.

Like most people, the author empathizes and knows how hard it is to recover from adversity and great misfortune. His popular "Losses, Lessons, and Blessings Cycle" course has changed his life and the lives of others. He thanks the Lord for his blessings and personally knows how gratitude, loyalty, forgiveness, and sharing can make a difference for people and for world peace.

Yes, He does have an eleven-year-old granddaughter, Emma.

Carpe Diem!

For more information on his Passport to Heaven products, speaking engagements, book signings, and seminars: email sirlouisp@gmail.com